1 MONTH OF
FREE
READING

at
www.ForgottenBooks.com

By purchasing this book you are eligible for one month membership to ForgottenBooks.com, giving you unlimited access to our entire collection of over 1,000,000 titles via our web site and mobile apps.

To claim your free month visit:
www.forgottenbooks.com/free924002

ISBN 978-0-260-04102-9
PIBN 10924002

This book is a reproduction of an important historical work. Forgotten Books uses
state-of-the-art technology to digitally reconstruct the work, preserving the original format
whilst repairing imperfections present in the aged copy. In rare cases, an imperfection in
the original, such as a blemish or missing page, may be replicated in our edition. We do,
however, repair the vast majority of imperfections successfully; any imperfections that
remain are intentionally left to preserve the state of such historical works.

BY

HIS EXCELLENCY

LEVI LINCOLN,

DELIVERED BEFORE THE

TWO BRANCHES OF THE LEGISLATURE,

JANUARY 8, 1833.

––––––––––

Boston:

DUTTON AND WENTWORTH, STATE PRINTERS.

....

1833.

2/4

ADDRESS.

Gentlemen of the Senate, and
of the House of Representatives:

THE political stations, to which, by the suffrages of our Fellow Citizens, we have respectively been assigned, for the coming year, and the duties of which, under the sanction of an appeal for our fidelity to the Searcher of Hearts, and with an invocation of the blessing of an overruling Providence upon our labors, we have now voluntarily assumed, devolve upon us high and solemn responsibilities. At this season of friendly salutation and personal good wishes, it is additional cause for mutual congratulation, and for devout and grateful acknowledgement to Heaven, that we enter upon the Trusts which have been committed to us, under circumstances favorable to their satisfactory discharge, in the fulfilment of the legitimate objects for which they were created. Witnessing, every where, in our beloved Country, the means of promoting private happiness, and the wide spread diffusion of the fruits of an unexampled national prosperity, the public Functionaries have but to regard the true sources of these enjoyments, and by a sacred observance

of the principles of patriotism, of social order, and of
moral virtue, to which they are referable, heeding the
admonitions of experience, and adopting the counsels of
wisdom, strive to secure their continued possession to the
improvement of their constituents, and their transmission,
as a rightful inheritance, for successive generations of
their Posterity.

In a review of the events of the past year, we cannot
fail specially to recognize the signal manifestation of di-
vine mercy, which has spared from the waste of a de-
structive Pestilence, the lives of the People of this
Commonwealth. While almost every other portion of
the habitable Globe has been scourged and agonized by
its ravages, and many of the Cities and Villages of our
own Country now mourn its terrible desolations, it has
passed lightly over us, leaving scarce an impress of its
fearful visitation. It may be, that, in the administrations
of an inscrutable Providence, we are yet to feel, still more
nearly, the admonitions which this Destroyer seems
commissioned to convey. Let it not be in vain, that,
even from a distance, it has taught lessons of precaution
in the wholesome ordinances of well regulated Commu-
nities, or given better assurance of individual security in
sober and virtuous lives. If, in the unregulated pursuits
of business, or the authorized indulgencies of society,
there are to be found inducing causes to a disease, which,
when once introduced, seizes for its prey, upon the useful
and the good, alike with the vicious and the worthless,
does it not demand the serious consideration of the Law-
giver and the Magistrate, how soon, and by what means,
these Causes may be controlled? An inordinate appe-
tite for the use of spirituous liquors, *too often gratified by
their free and unlicensed sale,* has given occasion for

immediate and greatest apprehension. If experience has shown, that, by moral influences alone, the former cannot be corrected, it becomes the more imperative, that, by wise enactments, and their rigid enforcement, the latter should be effectually restrained.

I have the satisfaction of advising you, that the domestic relations and interests of the Commonwealth continue to present the most gratifying aspect. There has been, during the past year, little for Executive attention, but the discharge of definitely prescribed duties, and that vigilant and faithful observance of the injunctions of the Constitution, and the provisions of Law, in the administration of the Government, which the fulfilment of the obligations of Office, in this Department, unceasingly requires.

In compliance with a Resolve of the last Legislature, upon the subject of certain Resolutions of the General Assembly of the State of Rhode Island, asserting a right to disturb the existing line of division between the two Governments, and to obtain possession and jurisdiction of a valuable portion of territory on our Southern border, an eminent Counsellor, one of the Senators of the State in Congress, was immediately consulted, and his professional services engaged, on the behalf of this Commonwealth. In a correspondence with him, I have been informed, that, at the last term of the Supreme Court of the United States, a Bill in Equity was filed in the name of the State of Rhode Island against Massachusetts, and the usual process moved for. As a question was then pending in a case between other parties, upon the power of the Court to sustain actions between States, without some Statute provision to regulate and aid the proceedings, no summons was issued. The granting of it, is now understood, to wait the decision, in the case referred to. Whatever may be the result of the application to the Court by the State of Rhode Island, an undoubting confidence may be entertained in the safe defence of Massachusetts against this extraordinary Claim. By investigations and discoveries of evidence, even since the able and satisfactory Report of the Committee of the Legislature of the last year, there is now placed, within the control of the Executive, additional, abundant, and, as it would seem, altogether unanswerable proofs, of the original establishment, and subsequent deliberate recognition and formal confirmation, by *both parties*, of the boundary line, in precise accordance with the actual possession of the territory on either side, and the practical jurisdiction, which, to the present day, has been exercised over it, by the Governments of the States, respectively. Undesirable, and indeed vexatious, under the circumstances, as litigation may be, there is no occasion on our part, for seeking to avoid it, through fear of the imputation of resisting the demands of justice, or from a reasonable apprehension of its unfavorable issue. Should the State be called into Court, it will not be without preparation to maintain, in sincerity and good faith, her position in the Controversy.

The disposition which was given by the General Government to the subject of the award of the King of the Netherlands, in relation to the North Eastern Boundary, involving so prejudicially the right of property in Massachusetts to the soil of the disputed Territory, superseded the occasion of any measures by the Executive of this Commonwealth, under the Authority of a Resolve of the 23d of March last. It may now be understood, from the advice of the Senate to the President, and the annunciation in his Message, at the opening of the present session of Congress, of a proposition having been made to the British Government to enter into a further negotiation upon the matter in dispute, that the opinion of the Arbiter is finally *rejected*, and the question restored to the true ground upon which it rested, prior to the submission. However unfortunate may be the occasion for a longer continuance of this controversy, yet confiding in the clear and distinct perception of the justice of the position, assumed, and uniformly and consistently maintained, by this Commonwealth, that the establishment of the line should be made to conform to the description of boundary given in the Treaty of 1783, by which, both the severance and sovereignty of the Nation were acknowledged, it may well be hoped, that the strenuous opposition and earnest remonstrances which were urged against the adoption of the compromise proposed by the Arbiter, will secure, in any future attempts at adjustment, a regard to the more precise and certain application of the terms of the Treaty to corresponding indications upon the face of the Country. No other mode of determination can be satisfactory. The value of the soil, as an object of property, has come to be better understood, and the weight of this interest to the States, added to the political advantages which jurisdiction over the Territory affords to the Nation, must forever, prevent its voluntary surrender. The refusal to accept the Award has been followed by no manifestation of hostility or disappointment on the part of the British Government. No new attempt has been made, during the year, by the neighboring Province, to extend its authority, nor by British Subjects, further to encroach upon our possessions, in this quarter.

In the management and disposal of other portions of

the public lands held by the Commonwealth, within the
State of Maine, the measures of the Land Agent have
been singularly judicious and successful. Pursuant to
the terms of a Convention entered into between the
Governments of Massachusetts and Maine, the situation
and description of all the lands, which were to be put
into the market, were carefully examined and ascertained, the Townships arranged into classes according
to their quality and supposed value, and the *minimum*
prices fixed for the regulation of the sales by the Agent
of each State. Under the authority of several Resolves,
the Agent of this Commonwealth has, in the course of
the season, disposed of twelve Townships of the divided
lands, lying in equal proportion on each side of the
Monument line, for the aggregate amount of *one hundred and thirty-four thousand, nine hundred and forty-
four dollars and thirty-seven cents*, and, in conjunction
with the Agent of Maine, bargained for the conveyance
of three Townships of the undivided lands, for a sum, of
which the Commonwealth's moiety is *thirty-eight thousand six hundred and ninety-nine dollars and ten cents.*
Sales have also been made of sundry small tracts and
detached parcels of land, remaining from former large
divisions between the States, and Permits granted, on
highly advantageous terms, for cutting timber, where the
fee of the land is still retained in the Government. By
all these proceedings of the Agent, within the year, not
less than *one hundred and eighty thousand dollars* will
probably be realized to the Treasury, while, from the
effect upon the remaining lands, of the increase of business and of settlement, induced by the opening of the
Country for occupation and improvement, it may well
be doubted, if the amount of the continuing interest of

the State in this property is, in any degree, diminished. When it is recollected, that, soon after the Act of Separation, a proposition was seriously debated in the Legislature, to dispose of *all* the right of the Commonwealth in the Public Lands, for a sum, less, even, than a few Townships, comprising hardly one *twentieth* part of the extent of the Commonwealth's title, have been sold for, in a single year, the immense value of this territory, and its future importance to the State as a resource for revenue, or a means of constituting a fund for the promotion of interesting objects, and permanent improvements at home, will be more justly estimated.

With the sales which have been made, the authority of the Agent, under former Resolves, has been exhausted. I now recommend an extension of his powers to the disposal of other tracts, which are favorably situated, and may be in immediate demand for their timber, or for settlement.

In addition to the sales which have been made, Bounty Deeds, conveying, each, two hundred acres, have been executed to seventy-three soldiers of the Army of the Revolution, or their legal representatives.

Such farther progress has been made in the construction of the Aroostook Road, that thirty-seven miles of the route are now completed. When it shall be carried through to the River, which the Agent anticipates may be by the close of another year, a region of great fertility, and abounding in the most valuable timber, bitherto excluded from approach, will be open to easy communication, and to the certainty of demand in the market, both for the lumber dealer and the settler.

In accordance with an arrangement authorized by a Resolve of the Legislature of the 23d of March last, the

Trustees of the Charity of Edward Hopkins have satis-
factorily executed and delivered, in the manner required,
a full and complete release of all claims and demands
in law and equity, upon the Commonwealth, and of
all claims and demands against the tenants of lands
in the towns of Hopkinton and Upton, of which
the Trustees claimed to be lessors, or successors
of lessors, and have been paid from the Treasury,
in consideration thereof, the sum of eight thousand
dollars. An occasion of controversy, which has long
vexed a portion of our fellow citizens, and often been
found troublesome and perplexing to the Government,
is thus, at length, happily put at rest.

The Trigonometrical Survey ordered by the Government, for the purpose of obtaining an accurate map of the
State, has been prosecuted, through the past season, and
is still in progress, under the direction, and by the personal
labors of the Civil Engineer, to whom the service was originally given in charge. From the monthly reports which
have been required of this Officer, there is continued
reason to be satisfied with his industry, faithfulness, and
skill, in the performance of this arduous and difficult task.
The perfect exactitude which is to be had in the observations and mensurations necessary to the triangulation, renders the process exceedingly slow, and, it is to be feared,
will occasion greater delay in the completion of the
work, than was at first anticipated. No map of like description has, as yet, been executed in any of the States;
nor is it known, that any such survey has before been
attempted in the country, except in the commencement
of a design by the General Government, some years
since, and now recently resumed, to procure, in like
manner, a Chart of the sea coast of the United States.

Since the undertaking here, the Legislature, for the time being, has been kept advised of its management and progress. All the Reports of the Engineer, general and special, up to the close of the last session, have been communicated by the Executive, and remain on the public files; and to these, are now to be added the special Reports for the past season, which will be transmitted. It has not been thought expedient to withdraw the Engineer from the country, while the weather remained open, for the purpose of preparing, for the present occasion, a more precise and connected account of his operations. This is a labor of time, and may be performed after the severity of the season shall have driven him from the field, and in sufficient opportunity to be presented to your notice during the session. It is confidently believed, that another year will complete the survey. But whatever may be the delay, this great work, when well accomplished, in connexion with the Map, and the Geological Survey and Reports embraced in the plan of the Government, will constitute an invaluable acquisition to the means of improvement, applicable alike, to the uses of the State, and the business of the citizens, and become a noble contribution to the promotion of the interests and cause of science.

The distinguished Professor, to whom was assigned the service of making the Geological Survey, and who, the last year, presented the first part of his Report, which has been given to the public, has now brought his interesting labors nearly to a close, and promises the result of his researches and observations, in the remaining parts of the Report, accompanied by numerous specimens of rocks, ores, and minerals, which have been collected and scientifically arranged and described, for the use of the Government, before the termination of your session.

A Commission, authorized by a Resolve of the 24th of February last, to revise, collate, and arrange the Colonial and Provincial Statutes, and the General Statutes of the Commonwealth, has been constituted, with an anxious regard to the character and importance of the service to be performed, by the appointment of gentlemen eminent as Jurists and Counsellors at law, who were conveniently situated for necessary, frequent, and free intercourse and co-operation with each other, and who have consented to enter upon this arduous and responsible trust. The Commissioners being required by the further provisions of the Resolve, " to suggest such contradictions, omissions, or imperfections as may appear in the laws to be revised, and the mode in which the same may be reconciled, supplied, or amended," have not had opportunity to make such progress in this extended work, as will enable them to report to the present General Court.

The provisions of a Statute of the last Legislature, for enlarging the jurisdiction of the Court of Common Pleas, and regulating the appointment and duties of prosecuting officers, have been carried into full effect, since the recess. As the law proposed an essential change in the administration of the criminal jurisprudence, and was considered, to some extent, an experiment, it is gratifying to learn, that it has proved, in a high degree, beneficial and satisfactory. Under the management of able and efficient prosecuting officers, the business of the Commonwealth has been disposed of in the Common Pleas, with great expedition, and but little if any interruption to the despatch of the civil docket, beyond what had been usual under the previous limited cognizance of criminal matters by this Court, while the Supreme Court, overburdened and oppressed as it still is, has been relieved from a portion of duty, which greatly interfered with the more important functions of a tribunal of appellate and final jurisdiction. Much loss of valuable time to the citizens, in their necessary attendance in the capacity of jurors, upon the Supreme Court, especially at the law sittings, is now prevented, and, from this cause, and also the shorter periods of the confinement of arrested persons, by the

terms of the lower Courts, a large aggregate of annual expense will, henceforth, be saved to the Treasury. Besides, as the administration of justice is prompt, the detection and punishment of offenders will be more certain, and crimes become less frequent.

In regarding the unquestioned advantages to the community, which have resulted from the operation of the recent law, I cannot but feel warranted in recommending to your consideration the expediency of modifying, still further, the distributive assignment of judicial

Pleas, in civil cases, subject to the right of appeal on exceptions in matters of law, and thus more equally apportioning the business between the respective Courts, by the convenient opportunity allowed to each, for its discharge. There appears no good reason why the issue of matters of fact, to be ascertained by a jury, composed of men of the same qualifications, and by a like mode of trial, should not be determined before the tribunal where they are made originally cognizable. When an appeal lies of right, it will too often be claimed with a view to the law's delay, or the supposed chance issue of litigation, rather than with reference to the character of the Bench, in the Court of ultimate resort. The Judges of the Supreme Court, it is well known, are now pressed to the most incessant and exhausting labors by the duties of their office, while a larger share of business, it is believed, might not unreasonably, nor unprofitably, be assigned to the Common Pleas. I respectfully submit to you, that the public interest requires the relief of the former, in the mode proposed, or in some more effectual and satisfactory manner.

The information will not fail to be received with great satisfaction by the Legislature, and the Public, that the noble Charity of a provision, in the construction of the State Lunatic Hospital, for the better care and treatment of the most abjectly miserable class of our Fellow Beings, is on the point of being made in readiness for their relief. The Government of the Institution has been organized, by the appointment of all the Officers authorized by law, and the adoption of by-laws for the regulation of its concerns, and I have been officially advised, that the Building will be prepared for the reception of those, who are to become its inmates, after the *tenth* day of the present month. A difficulty, however, has presented itself, under the Act providing for the regulation of the Hospital, passed on the 24th of March last, in respect to the removal of the Lunatics, who are now confined in the Gaols and Houses of Correction. By the 3d Section of that Statute, it is, among other things, enacted, " that as soon as the Hospital shall be prepared for the reception of the Lunatics, and that fact shall be made public by the Proclamation of the Governor, all Lunatics, who, at the time of such Proclamation, shall be confined in any Gaol, or

House of Correction, under any order, decree or sentence of any Court or any Judicial Officer, shall, *as soon as may be practicable*, be removed to said Hospital, under the direction of the Mayor and Aldermen of the City of Boston, or of the County Commissioners of the several Counties of the Commonwealth, at the expense of said City and Counties respectively." It has been represented to me by the Trustees, and indeed, it must be obvious from the dreadful nature of the malady, with which the persons to be removed are afflicted, that the reception of such numbers, at, or near the same time, would overwhelm with confusion and embarrassment every department of the Institution. " It will be utterly impracticable (say the Trustees in their communication) for the Superintendent of the Institution to receive, in one day, or even in a single week, all those insane persons, whose removal is peremptorily enjoined by the above mentioned law. But few individuals can be received and properly taken care of, in a day, without occasional hazard to the safety, and certain prejudice to the comfort, of each. Some time, also, will be required, for the Superintendent to learn the peculiar tendencies and disposition of each of the inmates, as preparatory even to an imperfect classification of the whole." From these considerations, the Trustees proposed, that directions should be given for the removal of the Lunatics, gradually, at different periods, and with sufficient intervals of time between the removal of those from different counties, to give opportunity for the convenient disposition of them, as they should arrive. Fully sensible of the propriety, and indeed, of the necessity, of such an arrangement, but doubting my authority, under the law, to require a conformity to it, I have delayed a Proclamation, that the subject might previously be submitted to your direction. In the mean time, that no neglect should occur in the improvement of the Institution, as soon, and as amply, as is admissible, a Circular letter has been transmitted to the Municipal and Executive authorities, who have the charge of removing the Lunatics, apprizing them of the time when the Building will be in preparation, and of the desirable arrangement in relation to the reception of its destined occupants. A copy of this Circular, containing a copy also of the communication addressed to me by the Trustees, will be laid before you. It will be observed, that these papers have regard, likewise, to the condition of the person and clothing of the Lunatic, at the time of his removal. This latter regulation is deemed of great importance to the future cleanliness, comfort, and success of the new Establishment. Under a view of all the circumstances, it remains to me, as a duty, to advise to an immediate amendment of the 3d Section of the Statute, so as to provide, instead of the requirement for the removal of the Lunatics from the Gaols and Houses of Correction, as *soon as practicable* after the issuing of the Proclamation, that they shall be removed, thereafter, from the Counties respectively, *in such time and manner, and with such previous preparation of clothing, as in the Proclamation shall be prescribed.*

The Commissioners, charged with the superintendence of the construction of the Hospital, have not yet had opportunity to collect the accounts of the expenditures, and prepare a Report of the progress and present state of the work, and of what remains to be completed. Various causes beyond their control, have contributed to delay them in the arrangement of the grounds, and the erection of the fences for the necessary yards to the seve-

ral departments of the Establishment. But the materials
are in preparation, and the whole labor may be accomplished, early in the ensuing season.

The visitorial and supervisory powers, which the Executive is required to exercise over the affairs of the
State Prison, necessarily make the condition of that Institution a subject of annual communication. The duty
of laying before you the Reports of its officers has never
been discharged with feelings of higher satisfaction, than
on the present occasion. With the former state of the
Prison, under arrangements which admitted of free intercourse and correspondence between the Convicts,
when little opportunity was afforded for moral culture,
and none for religious influences; when labor was compelled by privation and stripes, and industry induced by
the bribes of pernicious indulgence, the community have
long since been made acquainted. Humanity was shocked at the history of the abominations of the very place
set apart for the expiation of crime, and philanthropy
itself, well nigh despaired of the application of means to
produce correction. It was then, by a wise and liberal
act of legislation, involving in ultimate appropriations
nearly an hundred thousand dollars of expense, the experiment was commenced, of seclusion from association,
and employment in silence, of moral instruction, and religious admonition, encouragement, and consolation, of
which a degree of improvement in temper and character,
and in pecuniary results, even unlooked for in the most
sanguine anticipations, is already the certain and satisfactory result. In the congratulatory but modest language of the Inspectors, to whom so much credit for this
salutary change is justly due, " the Commonwealth
may be felicitated on the success of a system, at once

wise, humane and economical, affording to the convicts every possible opportunity and inducement for reformation, and, in the possession of an Institution, which, though it may be liable to some fluctuations, depending mainly on the price of labor in the vicinity, is yet, on the whole, competent to support itself, *permanently.* They have never held out higher expectations than these, in relation to it, and, after a careful observation of its progress, for more than four years, they do not hesitate to say, that these expectations are now realized."

In the early part of August, a disease, characterized in the Report of the Physician, as an "Epidemic Diarrhœa, attended with the greatest suffering and peculiar symptoms," suddenly broke out in the Prison, and, in the short space of twenty-four hours, prostrated more than one hundred of the convicts, reducing many of them, apparently, to the very point of death. "Then it was," says the pious Chaplain, "that every inmate of the Prison, however hardened and atheistical he may have before appeared, seemed to feel, that a mightier hand than any of mere created power was in the midst of them. Not a heart but quailed under the exhibitions of this power, which, as it were, in a moment, had prostrated, not the weakest merely, but the strongest and most hardy of their number. Not a soul but felt, that God was there !" And it was of the presence of God, in his blessing upon the application of human means, that all these lives were spared. Although the disease continued to prevail for weeks, and extended its attacks, with greater or less severity, to almost the entire number of Convicts, *not one* was suffered to perish. The assiduous and unwearied attention and successful skill of the Physician, aided by the gratuitous and kind offices of eminent medical men from the vicinity; the watchful superintendence of the Inspectors; the soothing ministrations of the Chaplain; the fearlessness, firmness, and devoted fidelity of the Warden and his subordinate Officers, in this trying period, deserve, that they should be borne in honorable mention to the Legislature.

The pecuniary accounts of the Prison, made up to the first of October last, show a balance of earnings and receipts, within the year, *exceeding, by four thousand, one hundred and ninety-two dollars and thirty-two cents*, the aggregate amount of expense, of every kind, incurred in the government and support of the Institution, and this, notwithstanding a great diminution in the number of Convicts, and the loss of more than *four thousand days labor*, by sickness. In the balance of credit, however, is included some amount for labor performed the preceding year, which has since been paid, but not more than an equivalent to the value of the time lost by the extraordinary Epidemic alone. To assist in forming a more satisfactory judgment of the industry, discipline, and good order of the Prison, and of the productiveness of its labor, it has been estimated by the Inspectors, that two hundred Convicts must earn, on an average, seventy dollars each per annum, besides their own support, to defray the charges upon the Institution, with the present number of prisoners.

I have but glanced at some of the most striking facts and results presented in the elaborate and interesting Reports from which they are gathered. If in doing even this, there may seem to have been too much of particularity, it should be considered, that the concerns of this Institution have heretofore been a subject of solicitous regard by the Government, and the moral condition of its inmates 'the occasion of deep feeling, throughout the Commonwealth. The experiment which has been making was important, both as a measure of Municipal regulation, and an attempt at Penitentiary reform, unpromising indeed in the beginning, and often discouraging in its progress, but the final success of which must be alike gratifying to the sympathies of human nature, and honorable to the character of the State in which it has been accomplished. The Reports will be found to contain many curious disclosures and valuable observations in relation to the causes of crime, in the neglected education and former habits and associations of the Convicts, and in reference to the means of correction, which are worthy the regard of the whole public. The history given by the Physician, of the appearance, prevalence, and treatment of the Epidemic disease, must be especially interesting to the cause of medical science.

The construction of a house for the residence of the Warden, within the limits of the Prison Yard, as directed by a Resolve of the Legislature, has been completed, and is now ready for occupation. Owing to a mistake of the Architect in the Plan approved by the Executive, an enlargement of the dimensions of the Building became necessary, after the contract for the work had been entered into, which has occasioned an inconsiderable excess of expenditure beyond the appropriation. The papers which will be laid before you, will explain the cause and amount of this difference, and the directions which were given by the Executive on the subject. A small additional appropriation will be required to satisfy the deficiency from the Treasury, or an authority to the Warden to retain the amount, from the balance of credit, in his accounts with the Prison.

The annual account of the state of the Treasury, made up to the first instant, exhibits a gratifying improvement in the condition of that Department. At the commencement of the last year, the balance of Cash on hand was $18,551 $\frac{3}{100}$. At the close of the year, it amounted to $81,223 $\frac{57}{100}$. This latter sum, however, is specially chargeable with the investment of $38,606 $\frac{24}{100}$, received for sales of Eastern Lands, which, by a standing order of the Legislature, is to be placed, as a distinct fund, on interest, subject to any future appropriations by the Government, and would reduce the balance to $42,617 $\frac{93}{100}$. The Receipts into the Treasury during the year, *including* the balance at its commencement, but *exclusive* of money borrowed of the Banks, and of all monies, whether for principal or interest, received on account of the lands, amounted to $384,141 $\frac{33}{100}$; and the aggregate of Payments, *exclusive* of money repaid to the Banks, to $304,613 $\frac{13}{100}$. Of the receipts, the sum of $74,507 $\frac{75}{100}$, was the proceeds of a State tax granted in 1831, which became payable into the Treasury the last year. If this sum also, should be deducted from the aggregate of receipts, as not resulting from the ordinary sources of Revenue, within the year, there would still remain $309,633 $\frac{58}{100}$, being an excess of $5,020 $\frac{39}{100}$, over the expenditures. By the aid of the tax, the debt of the Commonwealth to the Banks for loans, which have heretofore been required in anticipation of the Revenue, has been greatly diminished, and the large amount, now in the Treasury, produced.

On a comparison of the accounts of the two last years, it will be found, that the disbursements at the Treasury in 1832, were less, by $76,868 $\frac{49}{100}$, than in the year preceding. Unless disastrous public events should occur, to call for extraordinary expenditures, or interrupt the usual receipts, the revenue from provided sources, may safely be estimated as sufficient to meet the wants of the Government, without resort to a direct tax, the current year. Measures already in operation are effecting salutary retrenchments, and others which have hitherto unsuccessfully been attempted, may yet be adopted, with advantageous and saving pecuniary results.

In the above estimates, the still existing debt of the Commonwealth to Banks and Individuals for loans of money heretofore obtained, has not been disregarded. This debt is now reduced to $140,200 ; and with all the liabilities which are known to exist against the Treasury, the sum would not be made to exceed $30,000 more. Against this, the Commonwealth has the large Balance in the Treasury, of $81,223 $\frac{57}{100}$;—Stocks in notes of the Banks, upon the investment of money received of the United States on account of the Claim, to the amount of $281,000 ; and a further amount of $25,000 in special deposits bearing an interest of five per cent. on account of the sales of the public lands ;—together with Bonds, Notes, and Contracts, which are the securities for money, in payment for lands, to the amount of $170,812 $\frac{8}{100}$ with a still further sum of $10,845 $\frac{77}{100}$ in securities resulting from other sources ; thus making an aggregate of $568,881 $\frac{22}{100}$ in available funds, applicable, at the pleasure of the Government, to the discharge of obligations not exceeding, at the extent, $170,000, Future sales of land, and a further payment on account of the Claim, or, at least, the receipt of interest on that part of the principal which has been paid, are not such contingencies, but that they may reasonably be looked to;

as additional sources of supply to the Treasury of the State.

Much difficulty has occurred in the attempt to make a satisfactory investment of the money accruing from the sales of land, conformably to the order of the Legislature. The high prices of Stocks have been nnfavorable to their advantageous purchase in the market, and it is doubted, whether this would even be justified, while a right exists in the Government to subscribe to the Capital of the Banks. Yet, whenever the latter measure has been proposed, it has been met by the objection, that a subscription to the Stock of a Bank already in operation, by the addition of Capital, and the admission of a new partner, would necessarily occasion a valuation of all the property, and a settlement of the concerns of the Corporation, in order to determine the just proportion which the value of the old would bear to the new stock, and would otherwise be attended with such inconveniences as greatly to embarrass the business, and prejudice the interest of the Institution. Although the right of subscription, at any time, on the part of the Commonwealth, is too explicitly reserved in the Charter, to admit a question of the power to claim it, so strenuously have the objections to its exercise been urged, that a temporary arrangement for the deposite of $25,000, at an interest of 5 per cent. was consented to, until the more definite instructions of the Legislature could be had, on the subject. A considerable additional sum has since been accumulated in the Treasury, for the investment of which, the Treasurer now waits such instructions.

Previous to the close of the last session of Congress, an order was obtained in the House of Representatives, directing the Secretary of War to resume and proceed in the further examination of the Claim of Massachusetts for Militia Services during the late War, but the subsequent pressure of business in the Department, occasioned partly by the Indian War, and the multiplied and urgent applications under the Pension Act, and partly by the necessary absence of the Head of the Department from the Seat of Government during a considerable portion of the season, has delayed, until recently, any progress in the matter. It is now in the course of diligent and satisfactory attention, and will be urged, by the Agent of the State, to as prompt a determination as may consist with the opportunity for producing a proper understanding of the merits of the service, and securing a just allowance of the charges in the account.

A Bill, which passed both branches of Congress, providing for the payment of interest to the States, for monies advanced in measures for the common defence, during the War, and which would have given to Massachusetts and Maine, on that portion of the Claim which has already been liquidated and allowed, nearly *half a Million of Dollars*, failed to become a Law, through want of the sanction of the President's approval. In a Message addressed by him, at the present Session, to the Senate, where the Bill originated, his objections appear to have been taken to the form of the provisions, rather than to the principle of the enactment, and will doubtless be obviated by a new draft, to which they will not apply. A Bill to this effect has, indeed, already been introduced into the Senate, and, from the manifest equity which dictates the measure, reasonable confidence may be indulged, that it will now be permitted to pass into a law. It would be but a vain glorious boast, that the faith of the Nation was redeemed, by the extinction of the public debt, while the plainest obligation of duty remains to be performed, and the most common act of Justice is denied, to one of the Members of the Confederacy.

Recent experience has justified the apprehensions expressed to a former Legislature, of insecurity in the Plates used for the impression of Bank Paper. Close counterfeit imitations have been detected in circulation, and from their frequency of late, have created alarm for the credit of the currency. The business of society absolutely demands the utmost confidence in the purity of the circulating medium, and the possibility of its being corrupted should be guarded against by every precaution, which authority can impose. The Kalendars of our Prisons will show, that Counterfeiting, and passing Counterfeit Bills, have been among the crying sins of the land. The principal perpetrators of these offences are generally, the most ingenious and crafty of the Sons of Mischief, and from their extensive confederacies and associations, their detection is often dilatory and incomplete. In proportion as the evil is difficult of remedy, should be the vigilance exercised in means of prevention. A Report, by Commissioners having distinguished claims, from their general intelligence and their opportunities for practical observation, to public confidence, and who were appointed under the authority of the Government, with the ample scope of assigned duty, " to revise the laws concerning the form of Bank Bills, and the Plates from which they shall hereafter be impressed, and to report such other measures as may more effectually protect the Citizens of the Commonwealth against the forging and counterfeiting Bank Bills," re-

4

mains on the files of the last Legislature, and contains much valuable information and advice, with suggestions of alterations and amendments of the laws, applicable, in a twofold degree, at the present time, to this important subject. To this able and elaborate Document, I beg leave respectfully to refer your attention, alike for the facts and the arguments, which should induce to further provisions for the public security.

By an Act of the last Legislature, additional to " An Act to establish the Warren Bridge Corporation," the Executive was vested with certain powers, to be exercised upon the contingency therein provided for. As the Proprietors of the Bridge have since continued to collect the tolls, and no account has been rendered, by which it could be determined, whether they have been reimbursed the money to which they are entitled, an occasion for the interposition of the delegated authority has not, as yet, been presented. From the limitation of the operation of the Statute to the close of the present Session, some action must necessarily be had upon the subject, by this General Court. Of the disposition which should *ultimately* be made of the property, it is not my intention, at this time, to express an opinion. Should it be called for, hereafter, it will be formed according to the best of my understanding, with all the aids which legal authority and Legislative discussion may *then* afford, and whatever it shall be, it will be declared, upon an honest conviction, and with a single reference to the faithful discharge of official duty. But it should now be understood, that parties to a suit have appealed to the Tribunals of Justice, upon grave questions of Constitutional power, involved in the passing of the original Act of Incorporation, and it seems to me, that it would as little comport with a discreet regard to the possible future requirements of the public interest, as with a proper concern for private rights, and the respect which is due to the highest Judicial Tribunal of the Land, to whose Jurisdiction they have been submitted, to anticipate any decision, by an absolute and unchangeable measure of legislation. I therefore distinctly recommend, that, until the issue of the litigation to which I have refered, the Government should retain the same entire and unqualified control, which it now has, over the tolls and property of the Bridge, and should this issue not be had in season for more definite legislation the present Session, that the Act of the last Legislature should be extended and continued in force, for another year.

In the unequalled prosperity of the past year, the abundance of money, the facilities to credit, the excitements to enterprize, and the abundant rewards of labor, there is danger, that, both the adversity of former times, and the possible reverses of the future, may have been unheeded. A wise forecast will provide against the dis-

of view, measures, which have heretofore been proposed for the protection of creditors against fraudulent assignments by dishonest debtors, and the relief of honest but unfortunate men from the law's perpetual pressure, assume a new and increasing interest. My sentiments, on these subjects, have been fully and repeatedly submitted to the Legislature, but I should ill acquit a sense of duty, on the present occasion, if I neglected to urge the improvement of this favorable opportunity for a revision of the laws, that, by mitigating the rigor of their application to the person of the insolvent debtor, and securing an equal participation in the benefit of his effects to all who have given him trust, the just rights of property may be better protected for the one, and the dearer enjoyment of liberty, forfeited by no crime, made inviolable to the other.

The unavailing efforts hitherto made to produce reform, in the Constitutional representation of the People, might almost justify a distrust of the propriety of recommending a further attempt to this desirable end. Your practical experience, as constituent members of a legislative body of nearly *six hundred* Delegates, will now, present arguments of stronger personal effect, to direct your attention to the subject, than any which language can offer. The inconvenience of situation for the transaction of business; the difficulty of hearing or being heard in debate ; the interruption, confusion, and delays inseparable from the presence of excessive numbers in a deliberative assembly, are but too obvious to require relation. In these respects, the evil of a crowded representation is seen, and felt, and universally acknowledged. But here are the least of its objections. The absence of all feeling of individual responsibility for the measures of legislation, the greater danger of precipitancy, uncertainty, and incongruity, from sudden and popular influences upon its action, and the grievous burden of its expense, increasing and to increase with hardly any limits, do demand, that no opportunity should be omitted to press the strong necessity for a change. Efforts to produce it should never cease, until the work is accomplished. A spirit of personal disinterestedness and of public virtue, a clear perception of the requirements of duty, and concessions of mere preferences of mode, to the practicable attainment of the object, are alone necessary to secure success. No true friend to the best interests of the Commonwealth will contemplate, with satisfact on, a continuance of the existing state of things. Indeed, if it be not corrected, it must become more and more aggravated, until the people, impatient of the grievance, and having looked in vain to an application of the constitutional provision for relief, will, in their primary assemblies, declare, for themselves, the method of redress.

The unexpected delay, which took place the last year, in the passage of the Apportionment bill, by which the ratio of the federal representation is regulated, devolved upon the present Legislature the duty of providing for the election, in this Commonwealth, of Representatives to the next Congress of the United States. With the third of March next, the term of the twenty-second Congress expires, and it has already been publicly suggested, and the peculiar aspect of our domestic relations renders it not altogether improbable, that upon its dissolution, a new Congress may be specially convened. In even a remote prospect of such an event, a vigilant regard to the best interests of the State, would prompt to an immediate determination of the time and manner of choosing her Representatives. The most alarming present anticipations, could admit of no aggravation, beyond the apprehension of a meeting of Congress, in which Massachusetts might have no voice. Should there not shortly be more distinct indications of the course of future measures, it would seem to be demanded, by every consideration of political expediency and precaution, that the passage of a law should be hastened, providing for the choice of Representatives, and fixing the earliest convenient day for holding the elections.

With the present Legislature, also rests the responsibility of electing a Senator of the United States, after
the third of March next, when the term of one of the
Senators from this Commonwealth will expire.   In this
period of fearful apprehension for the stability of the
Republic, and of deep misgivings for the safety of our
free institutions, the whole people will expect, that the
influences of talent and eloquence, and learning, and
patriotism, which Massachusetts, in times past, with such
proud distinction to herself, and faithful service to the
Nation, has contributed to the support of the Constitution, and the maintenance of the integrity of the Union,
shall neither be withdrawn, nor in one jot diminished.

I have now, in the usual manner, and with as much
brevity as was consistent with a sense of obligation, presented to your view the prominent subjects of domestic
concern, which have fallen within the Executive Administration of the Government the past year, or seemed
proper to be suggested for the further advice and action
of the Legislature, at this time.   Happy would it have
been, if the duty of the occasion could have rested here.
But matters of more general and momentous import
demand your attention.   Dark and angry clouds, suddenly gathered, already appear high in the political
horizon, portending immediate and imminent danger.
A fearful tempest may be approaching.   A crisis, as extraordinary as it is unexpected, in our national affairs, is
at hand, and it behooves every true hearted citizen to
look well to the guards and securities, which wisdom and
patriotism and foresight have provided, for his own and
his country's safety.

The State of South Carolina, by its Chief Magistrate,
has formally transmitted for your attention, the proceed-

ings of a Convention of the Delegates of the people, in relation to the Tariff laws of the United States. By an Ordinance, deliberately and solemnly adopted in that body, these laws are declared to be unconstitutional, and, after the first day of February next, are abrogated and made null and of no effect, within the limits of that State, and all attempts to enforce them, by the General Government, are to be resisted with force and to blood. The powers and process of the Federal Courts, in the cognizance of matters concerning the revenue, or in the exercise of civil jurisdiction, in any wise touching its collection, against the citizens of the State, are prohibited, and the sanction of oaths required, and penalties enacted, to assure disregard and disobedience to their authority. In addresses by the Convention to the people of the State, and the citizens of the United States, which accompany the transmission of the Ordinance, the powers exercised by the General Government, are denounced as " gross usurpations." Measures deliberately adopted and pursued for years, with the sanction of a large majority of all the States, and people of the Union, are represented as " partial, unequal, and corrupt." The laws of Congress, passed at successive periods, and under many changes of representation, are declared to be " unparalleled for injustice and oppression under the forms of a free government." The whole protecting system is pronounced a " violation of the eternal principles of natural justice, converting the Government into a mere instrument of Legislative plunder," and in sustaining it, it is said, "the majority of Congress, is, in strict propriety of speech, an irresponsible despotism." It is further gravely charged, that, in relation to South Carolina, " all the powers of the earth by their commercial restrictions, and all the pirates of the ocean could not have done so much to destroy her commerce, as has been done by that very Government to which its guardianship has been committed by the Federal Constitution;"—that "a gigantic system of restrictions has gradually been reared up, and at length brought to a fatal maturity, of which it is the avowed object, and must be the inevitable result, to sweep that commerce from the great highway of Nations, and cover the land with poverty and ruin." And the people of all the States are admonished, "that the die is cast,"—that "South Carolina has solemnly resolved, that until these abuses are reformed, no more taxes shall be paid there;"—that she will "throw off this oppression at every hazard;" and will regard any attempt to enforce the laws declared by her to be null and void, "otherwise than through the civil tribunals, as inconsistent with her longer continuance in the Union,"—and finally, by requiring of Judges and Jurors an oath, "well and truly to obey, execute, and enforce" the Ordinance, she closes these tribunals against even this resort.

Such is a synopsis of the principles, measures, resolves, and threatenings, *in terms extracted from the Documents themselves*, which one of the States of the Union has sent forth, expressly for the notice and consideration, and impliedly, for the sanction of every other. Monstrous as they may appear, they are represented in no other or stronger character, than the elaborate arguments by which they are attempted to be justified, evince, they were intended to be understood. Called to pass upon this Bill of Presentment against a common Government, it will better comport with the cooler temperament of a section of Country, ungenerously taunted as

" the Manufacturing States, with an inhospitable climate and a barren soil," to examine the matter with calmness and deliberation, unexcited by the ardency of the appeal, and undetered from the performance of any patriotic duty, by threats of its consequences.

And is it then true, that we live under a Government which can deservedly be thus arraigned? Are we, wittingly and willingly, the slaves of a self-inflicted Tyranny? Is the policy to which we have so long submitted, and which has been so generally approved, injurious, partial, and corrupt? Are the tariff laws, repeatedly enacted by a Constitutional representation of the people, oppressive to the people, and repugnant to the Constitution? Where has the issue been joined? by what Court, Federal or State, from the first obnoxious statute in 1816, down to the present time, have these laws been adjudged void? What Carolina Jury would now pronounce them void, but for the Ordinance of Nullification; and why else this Ordinance, unless it be, to annul what otherwise might be held valid? No axiom in law is more universally understood, than that an unconstitutional enactment is a void Letter, absolutely, and in itself nugatory and without force. If the tariff laws are unconstitutional, it needed not the process of a Convention to absolve the people from obedience to them; but, if Constitutional, no Convention can destroy this obligation. The inequality and harships of a system, which the law upholds, are another and distinct consideration. These may be good causes for modifying or repealing, but not for disregarding a Statute. But to admit that a State may set at naught a law, which, however unacceptable, is in fact Constitutional, is to allow a party to the Federal Compact to violate, at pleasure, its own solemn engagements.

If the States, in their sovereignty, formed the Constitution, then did South Carolina, as one of them, agree, that the Laws of Congress, made in conformity to it, should be supreme. To disobey them, then, is to break the faith of that agreement. But if the whole people were the parties to the compact, the attempt of a State to annul the obligation, is an interference to prevent the execution of the laws, for which the violent and the lawless, under whatever form of combination they may seek to shelter themselves, are personally responsible.

But it is asked, shall the very power which claims to exercise a questionable authority, decide peremptorily upon its sufficiency? Certainly not. Nor shall he who derides that authority, be permitted to adjudge his own justification. The framers of the Federal Constitution foresaw, and wisely provided against this difficulty, and if the States, by subscribing to its terms, have conceded any thing, it is the clear, explicit, and exclusive right of judging of infractions of the instrument, in the making of laws, to the JUDICIARY. It betrays an unpardonable ignorance of the character of our Institutions to identify this department of the Government with the law-making power. The latter, within the scope of its legitimate exercise, is not more independent of the States, than is the Judiciary beyond the dictation of Congress. Both are the creatures of the Constitution itself, the work and the will of the people, each co-ordinate, distinct, disconnected from the other. It might as well become a State to abrogate a law, merely from a dissent to its expediency, as to usurp judicial functions in authoritatively pronouncing against its constitutionality. Whence too, the jealousy of this Tribunal? Has it manifested a want of independence; any spirit of subserviency to the Legislative or Executive Departments of the Government? On the other hand, has it not exhibited a noble elevation above the reach of all sinister influences, maintaining, through the strife of every party conflict, a fearless indifference to popular excitements, resting itself upon the consciousness of duty, and trusting for support to the intelligence of the people, the only enduring foundation of the fabric of free Government!

It is but a narrow view of the true policy of the protecting system, to regard it, only in connexion with the arbitrary and ever varying arrangements of men in the pursuits of business, or in its adventitious influences upon the local interests of different portions of the community. In its origin, it was, strictly, a Governmental measure. The revenue which it has produced, has hitherto been wanted for a purpose, to which the most uncompromising Anti-Tariff State will concede, that it might legitimately be applied. The Debt of the Nation is not, even yet, discharged, and, but for the duties, which have, either incidentally, or from intention in their imposition, afforded encouragement to Manufactures, would have now remained, to depress, with a millstone's weight, the struggling energies of the Country. Would South Carolina, think you, have consented, for its extinguishment, to have paid, by *direct taxes*, the Constitutional equivalent for her slave representation? And with what better propriety could she demand, that, to her exemption from this conventional proportion of the public burdens, the whole revenue of the Government should be raised by imposts, without discrimination as to objects, favoring in some degree, the interest of the non Slave holding States? But the protecting policy is to be sustained on higher grounds than the advancement of any local ob-

jects. Even its tendency to encourage domestic industry, and thus promote the prosperity and happiness of
the people, does not furnish the strongest argument in
its defence. It lies at the foundation of true National
Independence. It will enable the Country, in the ex-
tremest time of external pressure, to rest upon her own
resources, to disregard the Commercial restrictions of
other Nations, the cupidity of foreign monopoly, the ca-
priciousness of trans-Atlantic legislation. It will clothe
her Armies in War, and furnish supplies, occupation, and
necessary support to her people, under every emergency.
Let those who have heard, as has been heard,—aye, and
within these Halls too, a serious argument, eloquently
urged, against the improvident prosecution of a necessary war, from the inability of the Country to supply
Blankets to her Soldiers, estimate the genuineness of
that patriotism, which would again render an attempt to
vindicate National honor justly obnoxious to such an objection. If there be not enough in this latter consideration alone, to justify a tariff for protection, then, forth-
with, let it be abandoned. It is true indeed, that the
policy of encouraging domestic manufactures, by protecting duties, has of late been sustained, by the almost
universal sentiment of the people of this Commonwealth, and is defended by her entire Representation in
both Houses of Congress. It was not originally a New
England policy.... It was forced upon Massachusetts ;—
not voluntarily adopted by her. As recently as 1824, it
was opposed by the votes of all her Delegates, save
one. But from the decision of that time, it was regard-
ed as the established policy of the Nation, and has been
acquiesced in and conformed to, in all the arrangements
of business, until it has become so interwoven with the

pursuits of the People, that it cannot be surrendered, without wide spread and overwhelming ruin to the most valuable public interests. The course of domestic industry, thus directed and thus encouraged by the Government, now claims support, from its intrinsic importance, less to individuals than to the Community, to the extent of protection;—*efficient protection*, against disastrous competition, with foreign workshops, operated by the power of accumulated capital, bearing in other Countries, upon the labor of an oppressed and starving population. If beyond this, there has been aught of patronage or bounty, in the measures of legislation, prejudicial to any interest, let experience and discretion apply the remedy. This is a practical question, which, an enquiry into facts, rather than the speculations of political economists, will best determine. The Citizens of the " Manufacturing States," rugged as may be their soil, would, in the sweat of the brow, subdue it to the Hill tops, rather than seek, through a claim to exclusive privileges, peculiar advantages to themselves, to the denial of an equal right, in their Southern Brethren, to participate in all the sources of public and private prosperity.

But we are told, " the die is cast." Then be the consequences on the heads of those, who have recklessly risked all, which is dear in Country, upon the desperate hazard of the throw. The Government is the birthright of every citizen, established by the wisdom of a common ancestry, the progenitors of the present generation. It has carried the Nation onward, to a height of happiness, unexampled in the history of the world. Under the old Confederacy of States, separate in their absolute Sovereignty, it was weak, and feeble, and incapable of self preservation. Strength and prosperity sprung from "a more perfect union." They who would now violate this, are enemies to the peace and liberty of the land. Let none be deceived. *Resistance to the Union, is treason against the people!* There should no longer be reserve or disguise on this subject. This is not a time for indulgence in slothful security. The political watchman, who sounds not the alarm of danger, is sleeping on his post, or already, has betrayed his trust. They who say, that nullification may be made consistent with the preservation of the Union, are unsafe guardians of the public weal. They, who, with arms in their hands, pursue it, as a peaceable remedy, use but the mockery of words to conceal the true character of actions. Let South Carolina be conjured to pause, yet longer, before she strikes the parricidal blow. Opposition, by force, to the laws of the General Government, is REBELLION, from which the only escape is in REVOLUTION. Let her not lay hold of the very pillars of the Temple of Freedom, with the insane purpose, of burying the Country with herself, under the ruins of the beautiful and once hallowed Edifice. God grant, that better Counsels may save her.

For us, we have but to prepare for the trials and the duties, which the future may impose. The Chief Magistrate of the Nation has appealed to the whole People, to sustain, by the force of public sentiment, the sovereignty of the laws. Deprecating the occasion of a resort to force, he has, nevertheless, patriotically declared, that his duty is to the Country, and that this duty shall be performed ;—that the charge of administering the Constitution is a trust, delegated for the benefit of all, from which he cannot depart, at the bidding of a few. He has invoked the spirit of forbearance, consideration, and patriotism, among the Citizens of the disaffected State. He has appealed to them, by the remembrance of a common origin, a common Country ; by the sympathies of kindred and friendship ; and with assurances of security and happiness in continued Union, and the certainty of ruin and wretchedness in division and civil commotion. He has admonished them of the character and the consequences of their rash and precipitate measures, and he has entreated them, "as a Father," to retrace their steps, in the downward course to inevitable destruction. Thus far, the effort has been unavailing. Admonition has been met with scorn and defiance, and a summons to arms has answered the appeal to forbearance. It may even now be, that the irretrievable blow is given. Be it then ours, to rally to the defence of the Government and Laws. Let the response to the call of the Chief Magistrate be, the pledge of true hearts, and firm minds, and of the vigorous muscle of the freeman's arm, in support of the Constitution. If Nullification and Secession be suffered to obtain in a single State, the Union is no more. Each State, in its turn, will find cause of offence, and every occasion of dissatisfaction, will be but a fresh signal for revolt. The Constitution itself, will become, like the tempest broken vessel in the Ocean's storm, which for a while, may be upborne upon the billows, but must be cast, at last, in useless fragments, upon the strand.

It is consoling to turn from the threatening proceedings of one of the States, to the patriotic Resolves of another. Pennsylvania has transmitted, also, for your notice, the expression of her determination to stand by the Constitution and the Union. In Resolutions, which will be laid before you, she has asserted the supremacy of that Constitution, and of the Laws made in pursuance of it, over any pretension of reserved authority in a State, to absolve its citizens from their national allegiance She rejects the doctrines of Nullification, as an infraction of the vital principle of the Confederation; maintains the right of the General Government to impose duties upon imports, and to collect those duties in every part of the Union; and proffers the aid of all the means in her power, in enforcing the laws, and in sustaining the Chief Magistrate, in all Constitutional measures calculated to preserve and perpetuate the Union of the States.

Resolutions of the General Assembly of the State of Tennessee, disaffirming the powers of the General Government to make internal improvements within the States, without their consent, and approving the views and sentiments of the President as expressed to Congress in his negative upon the Maysville Road Bill, and Resolutions in relation to the disposition of the public lands, recommending the appropriation and distribution of the nett proceeds of the sales, among the States and Territories, as a fund for Education, are also submitted to you.

Permit me, Gentlemen, in conclusion of this already too protracted Address, to add one word of personal reference. The honor, which has been conferred upon me by my Fellow Citizens, in numerous successive elections to this high station, has claims to acknowledgements, which I have power but feebly to express. It were better, that my earnest, though humble efforts, to requite the confidence reposed in me, should now be appealed to, to testify the sincerity and depth of that gratitude, which a just sense of the obligation has inspired. The ensuing year will complete the ninth term of my Executive Office. During this long period, a generous indulgence has been uniformly extended to me by the People, and a faithful, efficient, and friendly support, without which that indulgence could not have been looked for, accorded by those, with whom it has been my happiness to have been officially associated. Sensible to the dictate of Republican principle, which demands, in elective offices, the occasional freshness of new powers for the public service, and by a change of *Men* presents to *all*, the highest incentives to deserve the public honors, I now beg leave, to announce my intention, to decline being considered a Candidate for re-election. If, at the close of the year, it shall be permitted to me, to see this ancient and beloved Commonwealth, the Land of the sepulchres of the Pilgrims, and of the monuments of the virtues of Sages and of Patriots, then united, as it now is, in public sentiment, rejoicing as it now does, in unsurpassed prosperity ; to carry with me, into private life, some portion of the regard of my Fellow Citizens, which has cheered the path of official duty ; and thereafter, to share in the kind remembrance of those, whose councils have aided in the public service, that voluntary retirement from office, to which I have constantly looked, may not have been delayed, too long. Let it be remembered by us all, that, whether in public or private stations, high personal responsibilities will continue to attach to us. As Citizens of the only Republic on earth, we have a trust, such as was never before committed to any people. With us, rests the keeping of the Ark of the Covenant of Civil Liberty. Here, in these United States, are those alone, who bear it. The hopes of the World are upon us. The prayers of the oppressed of all Nations are with us. Let us be true to ourselves ;—true to our duties ;—true to the destinies which are in our own hands,—firmly resolved, in the possession of the blessings which a kind Providence has vouchsafed to us, that they shall go down to our Children, sealed, even, if it needs must be, with the blood of their Fathers.

LEVI LINCOLN.

State House,
Boston, Jan. 8th, 1833.